L.E.A.R.N. WHAT PAP KNEW

THE GRAPHIC NOVEL

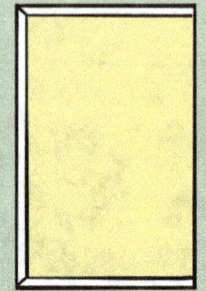

The SHOP SECRET: L.E.A.R.N. What Pap Knew

Jim Carbaugh

©2024 All Rights Reserved. No portion of this book may be reproduced, stored
in a retrieval system, or transmitted in any form or by any means—electronic, mechanical, photocopy,
recording, scanning, or other—except for brief quotations in critical reviews or articles without the prior
permission of the author.

Published by Game Changer Publishing
Paperback ISBN: 978-1-965653-38-8
Hardcover ISBN: 978-1-965653-39-5

L.E.A.R.N. WHAT PAP KNEW

THE GRAPHIC NOVEL

WRITTEN BY JIM CARBAUGH, M.ED
ILLUSTRATED BY DORI DURBIN

THEY LOVED THIS BOOK, TOO.

In "The Shop Secret: L.E.A.R.N." Jim Carbaugh delivers a story that is both practical and universally relevant for all classrooms. By blending essential life skills with an engaging storytelling format, the book resonates with readers of all ages. The L.E.A.R.N. principles—Listen, Ethics, Attitude, Respect, and No—are not only timeless but should be integral to every educational environment, from preschool to post-graduate studies. Jim's insights are applicable across all stages of life, offering lessons that will leave a lasting impact. His ability to connect with readers through a relatable family story is a testament to his skill both as an educator and a storyteller.

Jack Appleby
Retired Teacher, Principal, Superintendent, Educational Consultant

The "Shop Secret: L.E.A.R.N What Pap Knew" was a wonderfully told story that students at any age can relate to. A story about a grandfather and his grandson is just what children need to read in a time with few traditions and families still intact. All of the ideas Pap shared are the essential skills needed in the workforce, as well as, strategies for children to be successful in school. In my role as a school counselor in a middle school, I will use this story when students are struggling academically, behaviorally and even emotionally.

Tammy Lee
School counselor and Mom
Tuscarora School District

The 'Shop Secret: L.E.A.R.N. What Pap Knew" by Jim Carbaugh is a heartwarming and inspiring book that delivers timeless wisdom for all readers. Through the tough love relationship between a grandfather and his grandson, Jim, students are introduced to the essential values of Learning, Ethics, Attitude, Respect, and how to think through saying No. This book offers a powerful framework that resonates with students in grades 5-12, helping them navigate life with confidence and purpose. Highly recommended for educators and students alike, it provides practical lessons on success and character building that will last a lifetime.

Tom Durbin
Secondary Principal
Hudson Area School

"The Shop Secret: L.E.A.R.N. What Pap Knew" offers a heartfelt blend of family values and practical wisdom in a visually engaging graphic novel format. Through the touching relationship between a grandson and his grandparents, readers are introduced to important lessons about patience, hard work, and respecting others. This book, with its accessible storytelling and interactive workbook pages, is sure to help middle-grade students reflect on the importance of character and the guidance trusted mentors can provide.

Erin L. Faulkner
Librarian, Mountain View Middle School

...SO DID THEY.

Amazingly paced with simple and concise storytelling. A wonderfully clear 'life lesson' learned but it goes much deeper than that on an emotional level. Pap was truly an amazing man who reminds me of my own grandfather, (but without the thick Italian accent). It was a privilege to read and a good reminder of how there is always more to learn and how a good attitude will always gain good results.

Billy Tucci
Creator and Publisher at Crusade Comics

Jim Carbaugh's book "The Shop Secret" is engaging, relevant and easy to relate to. This book is valuable for all ages, providing principles for life that are bound to create successful outcomes. What sets this book apart is the storytelling and how relatable it is – most people get great lessons from their grandparents, and what Jim learned from his pap embodies this.

Liam Sandford,
Best Selling Author of Effortless Public Speaking

DEDICATION

To the readers of "The Shop Secret: What Pap Knew:"

This story is dedicated to all the dreamers, learners, and those who seek to make a difference in their lives and the lives of others. It is a testament to the power of wisdom passed down through generations and the journey of discovery we each must undertake.

At the heart of this journey are the "L.E.A.R.N. Principles" —a guiding force that can help you unlock your true potential and achieve your life's goals. These principles are more than just words; they are a blueprint for success, growth, and fulfillment in everything you do.

As you immerse yourself in this story, remember that Pap's wisdom and these principles can be applied to your own life. By embracing them, you can take charge of your journey, rise to challenges, and reach the goals that once seemed out of reach.

May this novel inspire you to "L.E.A.R.N." and lead you toward the future you envision.

With gratitude and hope for your journey,
Jim Carbaugh

FOREWORD

It's not often you come across a story that is both deeply personal and universally resonant. *The Shop Secret: L.E.A.R.N. What Pap Knew* is exactly that. Jim Carbaugh has crafted a narrative that takes the reader on a transformative journey into the heart of mentorship, wisdom, and the values that shape us into who we are.

In this graphic novel, those principles come alive through Pap's life lessons, shared with his grandson in the most unexpected of places—a humble shop. Their conversations are more than just dialogue; they're reflections of the kind of mentorship that transcends generations, where wisdom is passed down in the most practical and impactful ways.

Jim's storytelling is infused with the same authenticity and heart that he brings to his work and also his friendships. His ability to weave complex ideas into simple, actionable principles is a gift, and this book is no exception. As someone who values the importance of leadership and personal growth, I see The Shop Secret as not only a powerful story but also a practical guide for anyone looking to inspire personal growth and navigate life with integrity, empathy, and purpose.

As you turn these pages, you'll not only be entertained but also invited to a journey of self-discovery. What are your core values? Who are your mentors? And what do you, in turn, pass on to others? These are not just questions but invitations to reflect on your journey and the impact you can have on others.

Pap knew the answers to these questions, and by the end of this book, you'll find yourself closer to understanding them too.

Cesar Cervantes
Founder, Top Talks
TEDx Speaker
Speaker Coach & Speechwriter

It was Sunday and my first week back from college. I had just finished going to the gym and decided to stop by my grandparents' house. As soon as I got there I headed to the back porch and there was my grandmother, 'Nana.' She was enjoying the great mid-May sun.

SUNDAY

"Hey there!"

WHAT DID YOU "L.E.A.R.N." ABOUT...

At the end of each chapter there is a spot for you to reflect and act on what you have L.E.A.R.N.ed.

Please use these spaces to get your ideas flowing and share what you know!

List three people you would consider to be your mentors or people you enjoy learning from:

List three people who you would LOVE to learn something new from:

WHAT DID YOU "L.E.A.R.N." ABOUT...

What are three ways you can start to improve your listening skills?

How can you help others improve their listening skills?

WHAT DID YOU "L.E.A.R.N." ABOUT...

What are the top three values you look for in a person?

List the three top values you were known for:

What are your top three non-negotiable values overall?

WHAT DID YOU "L.E.A.R.N." ABOUT...

What are three ways you can keep a positive attitude?

When you were confronted with a negative situation, how did you turn it into a positive outcome?

How can you help others maintain a positive attitude?

WHAT DID YOU "L.E.A.R.N." ABOUT...

How can you show respect towards others?

How can others show respect towards you?

WHAT DID YOU "L.E.A.R.N." ABOUT...

When receiving a no, what are ways you can move forward?

No, it is not the end, but the beginning. What does this statement mean?

When you have to say NO, what can you use to help the others move on?

"L.E.A.R.N." is not JUST a word. It's what you need to do every single day. Every day you can:

L — LISTEN UP BEFORE YOU SPEAK UP

E — ETHICS; DO THE RIGHT THING AND ADD VALUE.

A — ATTITUDE; KEEP IT POSITIVE

R — RESPECT EVERYONE. TREAT HOW THEY WANT TO BE TREATED.

N — NO EXCUSES. OWN IT. SOLVE IT.

L.E.A.R.N. and you will succeed in all you do!

ABOUT THE AUTHOR

Jim Carbaugh is a seasoned TEDx speaker, distinguished educator, and revered coach with over forty years of experience guiding individuals, schools, teams, and organizations toward excellence. With a deep-rooted passion for the outdoors, Jim infuses his work with the wisdom of nature, creating transformative experiences for his clients and audiences alike.

As a co-author and graphic novel author, Jim's storytelling prowess transcends traditional leadership narratives, offering fresh perspectives and profound insights. He is a certified member of the John Maxwell team and embodies the highest standards of leadership excellence in his practice.

Jim Carbaugh, in addition to his roles as an educator and author, is the visionary founder and CEO of All Points Leadership, a renowned firm dedicated to cultivating exceptional leaders and fostering thriving organizational cultures. His innovative L.E.A.R.N. Principles of leadership and culture development have not just evolved but revolutionized the way individuals and teams approach growth and transformation.

With a relentless commitment to empowering others, Jim Carbaugh continues to inspire, educate, and guide individuals and organizations worldwide on their journey toward success and fulfillment.

ABOUT THE ILLUSTRATOR

Dori Durbin is a Christian wife, mom, children's book author, illustrator, book coach, ghostwriter and podcaster of "That's Good Parenting" who after experiencing a life-changing illness, left a secondary teaching career and followed her passion for creativity and fitness.

Now she impacts kids and parents through writing kids' books. Dori wrote her "Little Cat Feelings Series" for kids and parents to emotionally connect earlier in life. Her true passion is coaching and illustrating books for experts and authors who also want to impact families earlier in life with their kid-sized expertise packed into purposeful and fun kids' books.

www.ingramcontent.com/pod-product-compliance
Lightning Source LLC
Chambersburg PA
CBHW072003060526
44107CB00150B/335